Igneous ROCKS

Hit the road and discover a world that rocks!

Published in 2025 by **Cheriton Children's Books**
1 Bank Drive West, Shrewsbury, Shropshire, SY3 9DJ, UK

First Edition

Author: Sarah Eason
Designer: Paul Myerscough
Editor: Deborah Jones
Proofreader: Katie Dicker

Picture credits: Cover: Collaborate; Inside: p1: Shutterstock/Joenk, p4: Shutterstock/www.sandatlas.org, p5: Shutterstock/Withan Tor, p6: Shutterstock/Vadim Sadovski, p7: Shutterstock/Ashish Wassup6730, p8: Shutterstock/ImageBank4u, p9: Shutterstock/Yuriy Buyvol, p10: Shutterstock/ARoxoPT, p11l_NASA, p11r_Ministry of Land, Infrastructure, Transport and Tourism, Japan, p12: Shutterstock/Aleksandr Pobedimskiy, p13: Shutterstock/Shawn Zhang, p14: Shutterstock/Photo World, p15: Shutterstock/RHJPhtotos, p16: Shutterstock/Mopic, p17: Shutterstock/Attila Jandi, p18: Shutterstock/Yes058 Montree Nanta, p19: Shutterstock/Maximillian Cabinet, p20: Shutterstock/The Wild Eyed, p21: Shutterstock/Tamara Kulikova, p22: Shutterstock/Marcel Clemens, p23: Shutterstock/Alexander Demyanenko, p24b: Shutterstock/Paul Atkinson, p24t: Shutterstock/Stas Malyarevsky, p26: Shutterstock/Pecold, p27: Shutterstock/Svetlana Bondareva, p28: Shutterstock/Santi Rodriguez, p29: Shutterstock/Sergii Figurnyi, p30: Shutterstock/Antstang, p31: Shutterstock/Jason Patrick Ross, p32: Shutterstock/Irina 1 Nikolaenko, p33: Shutterstock/Vitpho, p34: Shutterstock/Miss Ty, p35: Shutterstock/Carlos Aranguiz, p36b: Shutterstock/Jen Watson, p36t: Shutterstock/Bjoern Wylezich, p38: Shutterstock/Mazur Travel, p39: Shutterstock/Rui Serra Maia, p40: Shutterstock/Andrew Mayovskyy, p41: Shutterstock/Yvonne Baur, p42: Shutterstock/Pedal to the Stock, p43: Shutterstock/Evgeny Haritonov.

Printed in China

Please visit our website,
www.cheritonchildrensbooks.com
to see more of our high-quality books.

CONTENTS

Chapter 1 **Our Rocky World** 4

Chapter 2 **Igneous Stars** 8

Granite—What a Rock Star! 12

Chapter 3 **Rising Up** 16

Basalt—What a Rock Star! 18

Pumice—What a Rock Star! 24

Chapter 4 **An Igneous World** 26

Gabbro—What a Rock Star! 32

Obsidian—What a Rock Star! 36

The Road Trip Guide to Rock Hunting 42

The Rock Cycle Road Trip Quiz 44

Glossary 46

Find Out More 47

Index and About the Author 48

Chapter 1

Our Rocky World

Our planet is made almost entirely of rock. It has a small metal core at its center, but the remaining 85 percent of it is rock—and that's why it is so easy to find many amazing rocks on Earth.

All Change

Although the rocky surface of our planet may seem stable, it is being reshaped and reformed all the time. Sometimes, changes to its surface can happen quickly. For example, because of a natural disaster such as a landslide or earthquake. Most of the time, the changes to Earth's rocky surface happen very, very slowly—so slowly that we hardly notice them. Over a very long period, surface rocks are broken down to make way for new rocks. This is part of a never-ending cycle called the rock cycle.

When magma reaches Earth's surface it is called lava. It cools, hardens, and forms igneous rock.

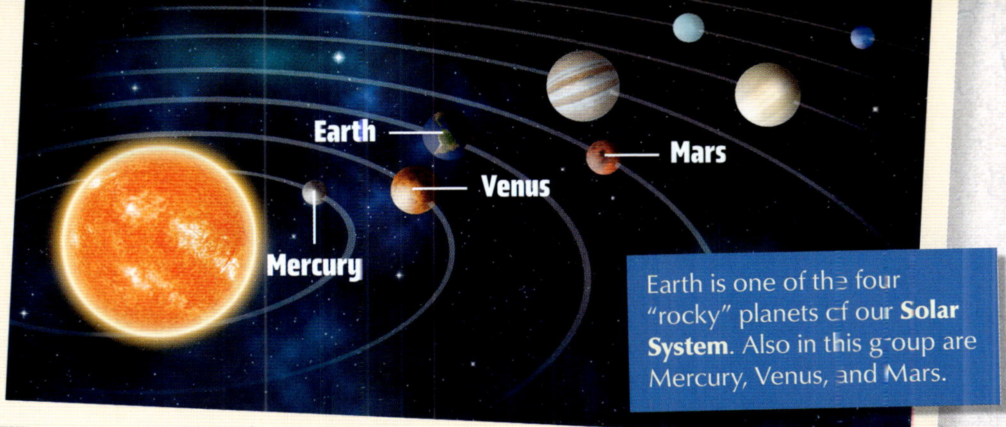

Earth is one of the four "rocky" planets of our **Solar System**. Also in this group are Mercury, Venus, and Mars.

Earth's Rock Cycle

The rock cycle is a process by which one type of rock changes into another type of rock. Earth has three main types of rock: igneous rock, metamorphic rock, and sedimentary rock. Each can change into another type when affected by temperature, **weathering**, and **pressure**.

How Rock Changes

When heated deep underground, rocks turn into liquid rock. We call this melted rock magma. When rocks are worn away by weathering or **erosion**, they break into smaller pieces called sediment. Rock can also be squeezed under great pressure, which also forces it to change.

Understanding Rock Types

Igneous rock is magma that has cooled and hardened. This can happen above or below the ground. Igneous rock changes by melting into magma, eroding into sediment, or being pressed so tightly that it becomes metamorphic rock.

Metamorphic rock began life as igneous or sedimentary rock that was then heated and squeezed. Metamorphic rock can change again by eroding into sediment or melting into magma.

Sedimentary rock is made up of squashed sediments from other rocks, plus the remains of living things. It can erode back into sediment, be squeezed into metamorphic rock, or melted into magma.

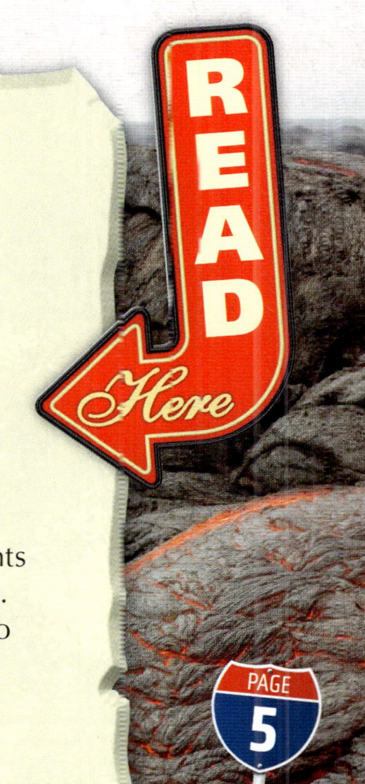

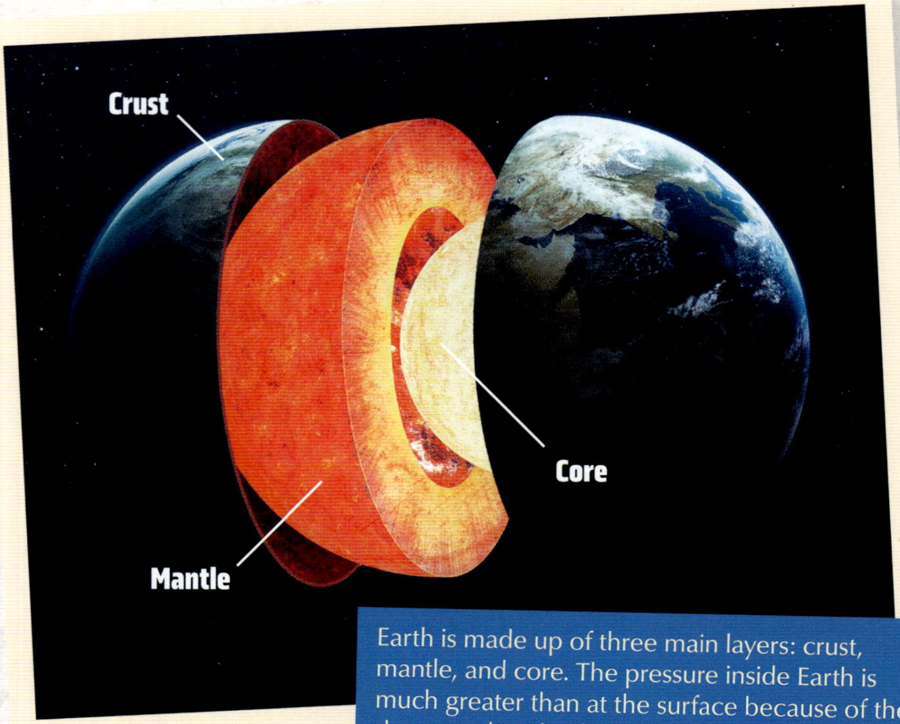

Crust
Core
Mantle

Earth is made up of three main layers: crust, mantle, and core. The pressure inside Earth is much greater than at the surface because of the downward push of millions of tons of rock above.

Look Inside Earth

To understand the rock cycle and why rock is so affected by temperature, weathering, and pressure, we need to first look at the structure of Earth.

Earth looks solid and immovable at the surface, but inside are layers that are not at all like the surface. In fact, Earth is made up of three very different parts.

Crust: This is the outer part of our planet. It is the section on which we live. It is up to 44 miles (70 km) thick and is broken up into enormous parts, called plates.

Mantle: This mostly solid layer moves around and is about 1,800 miles (2,900 km) thick. Earth's plates float on the mantle.

Core: This is the hottest part of our planet and it forms the center of Earth. The center of the core reaches nearly 12,000 degrees Fahrenheit (6,700 °C), hot enough to keep it permanently molten, or liquid.

Rock Recycling

During the rock cycle, new rock material can rise to the surface from deep within Earth. But most surface rocks are made from existing rock that is continually recycled. For example, as a rock is weathered, a grain within it may be loosened. That grain may then become part of another rock. It will then be weathered and separated from that rock, and form part of a new rock, repeatedly.

Take a Rock Cycle Road Trip!

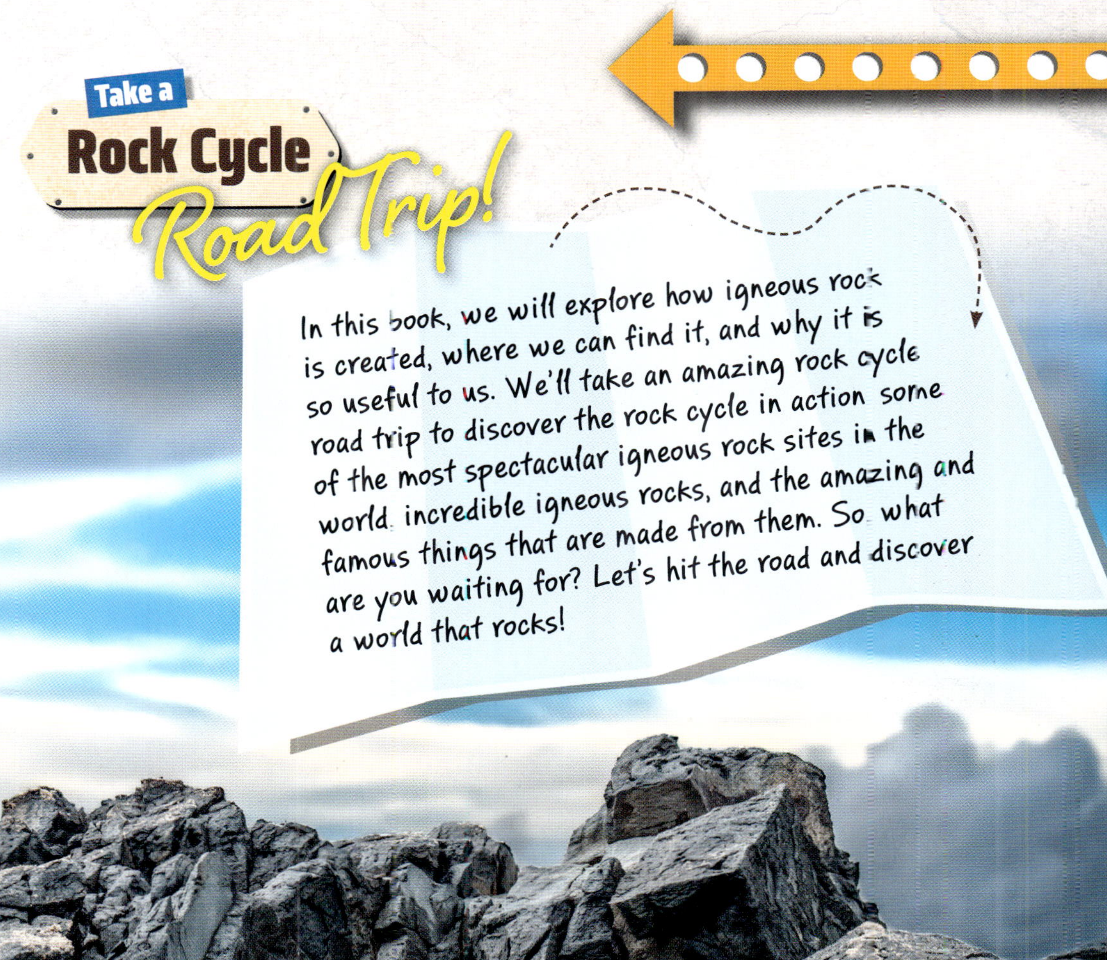

In this book, we will explore how igneous rock is created, where we can find it, and why it is so useful to us. We'll take an amazing rock cycle road trip to discover the rock cycle in action some of the most spectacular igneous rock sites in the world incredible igneous rocks, and the amazing and famous things that are made from them. So what are you waiting for? Let's hit the road and discover a world that rocks!

Igneous rocks tell stories about Earth's never-ending rock cycle.

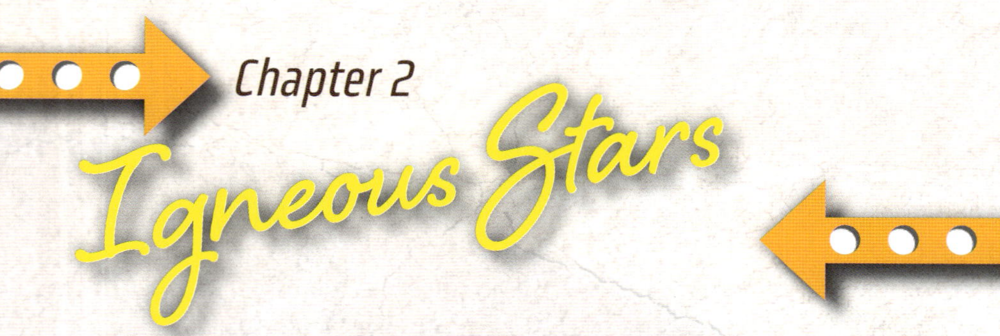

Chapter 2

Igneous Stars

Have you ever seen hot wax run down the side of a candle and set hard as it cools? Igneous rock forms in the exact same way—but from magma. The word "igneous" means "formed through fire."

Made by Magma

Volcanoes are cracks in Earth's crust, and inside volcanoes there is red-hot, liquid magma. When volcanoes erupt, magma reaches Earth's surface, where we call it lava. It cools quickly and hardens into new igneous rock. However, when magma rises through gaps that do not reach the surface, it cools more slowly and forms other igneous rocks beneath Earth's crust.

Once magma reaches Earth's surface it may flow across it like a river.

Digging Deeper

The grains that we see in rock are **crystals**. Crystals form when molecules in a liquid gather when that liquid begins to cool and harden. The size the crystals grow to depends on how quickly the liquid cools and hardens. Crystals have more time to grow when a liquid cools and hardens slowly, and less time to grow when it cools and hardens quickly.

READ Here

Getting Hotter, Getting Cooler

Magma can reach temperatures of around 2,200 degrees Fahrenheit (1,200 °C). It rises into holes and cracks in rock above it, a little like a hot-air balloon rises through the surrounding cooler air. Once the magma can rise no farther, it starts to cool. It cools slowly, over thousands or even millions of years. This is because the rocks that surround the magma deep underground are still much hotter than those at the surface.

Big and Small

Some igneous rock, such as granite, has large grains inside. Other rock, such as basalt, has tiny grains. The size of the grains are clues to how they formed. Large grains need longer to grow, so they formed while the magma was slowly cooling underground. Basalt has tiny grains because it formed from fast-cooling lava.

The Igneous Stars

There are many igneous rocks on Earth. Some of the best known are granite, basalt, pumice, obsidian, gabbro, tuff.

Underwater volcanoes can result in the formation of dramatic-looking islands and rock formations, like this islet off the coast of São Miguel in the Azores, Europe.

Pushy Rock

One of the simplest differences between igneous rocks is whether they formed at the surface or underground. Those that formed underground are called intrusive rocks. That is because the magma intruded, or pushed, into rock above it.

Made of Minerals

All rocks are made from one or more **minerals**. In a rock, the minerals are solid. However, in magma, they have melted and bonded together. When magma cools, the different minerals in it each start to form solid, regular-shaped crystals. Granite is one of the most common intrusive rocks. It is usually made up of crystals of clear quartz, white or pink feldspar, and dark brown biotite minerals.

Digging Deeper

Some mountains that tower over the land today are made from intrusive igneous rock that formed underground long ago. Over thousands or millions of years, the softer rock above them was gradually weathered by chemicals in rainwater, by wind and ice, and by temperature changes that cause the rock to expand and contract. The weathered pieces of soft rock were eroded by moving water and wind. The harder igneous rock remained because it weathers more slowly.

Take a Rock Cycle Road Trip!

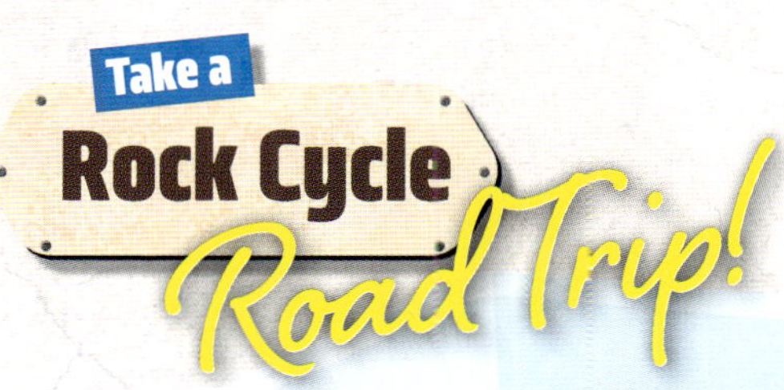

In 2013, a new island made of volcanic rock appeared in the sea off the coast of Japan. This new igneous rock formed due to the **eruption** of a deep-sea volcano. It's the first stop on our road trip. Head this way!

ROCK STOP! NISHINOSHIMA, ASIA

The island lies about 600 miles (970 km) south of the Japanese city of Tokyo, in Asia. In 2013, a NASA **satellite** captured images of the island, which had risen from a volcanic eruption. By 2014, the island had grown to about 13.8 acres (56,000 sq m) and had risen 55–82 feet (20–25 m) above sea level, growing big enough to join up with another nearby island, Nishinoshima. Scientists think that the island could keep growing for a few more years.

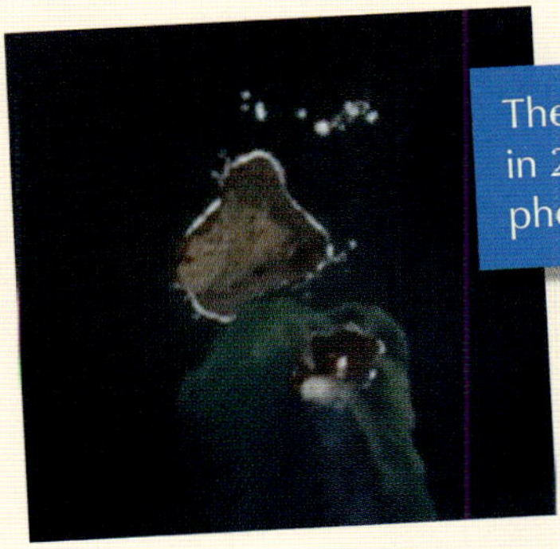

The photograph on the left shows the new island in 2013 (bottom) next to Nishinoshima (top). The photograph below shows the joined islands in 2018.

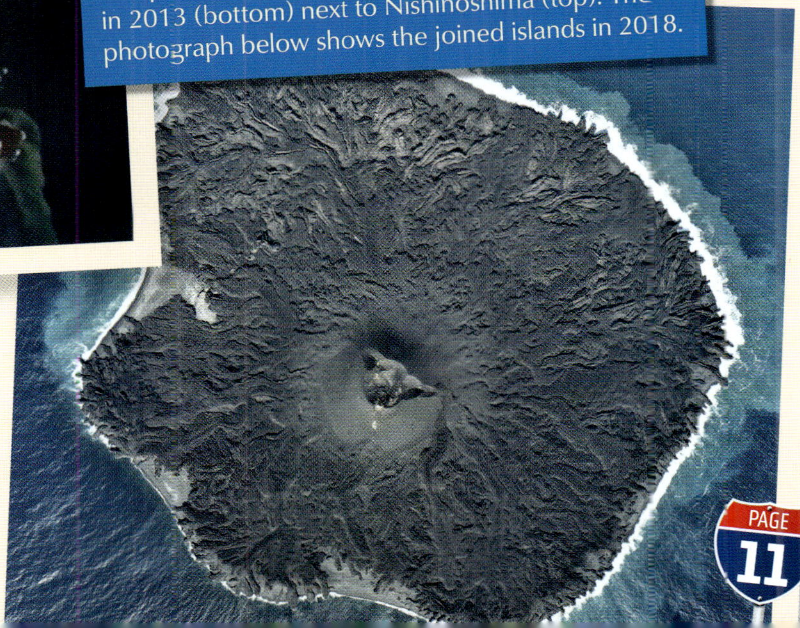

GRANITE

What a Rock Star!

Granite is possibly the best-known igneous rock. That is because granite is used in so many everyday objects, from floor tiles and kitchen countertops through monuments and paving stones. Granite is all around us!

THAT ROCKS!

Granite is one of the hardest substances on Earth. It is very difficult to mark, which makes it an ideal material for worktops, paving, and garden ornaments.

Rock Star Characteristics

- Often red, pink, gray, or white in color with dark grains
- Grains are large enough to see without the aid of a microscope
- Very hard but can be polished to create a gleaming, shiny surface

The United States has many natural granite landmarks, such as Stone Mountain in Georgia.

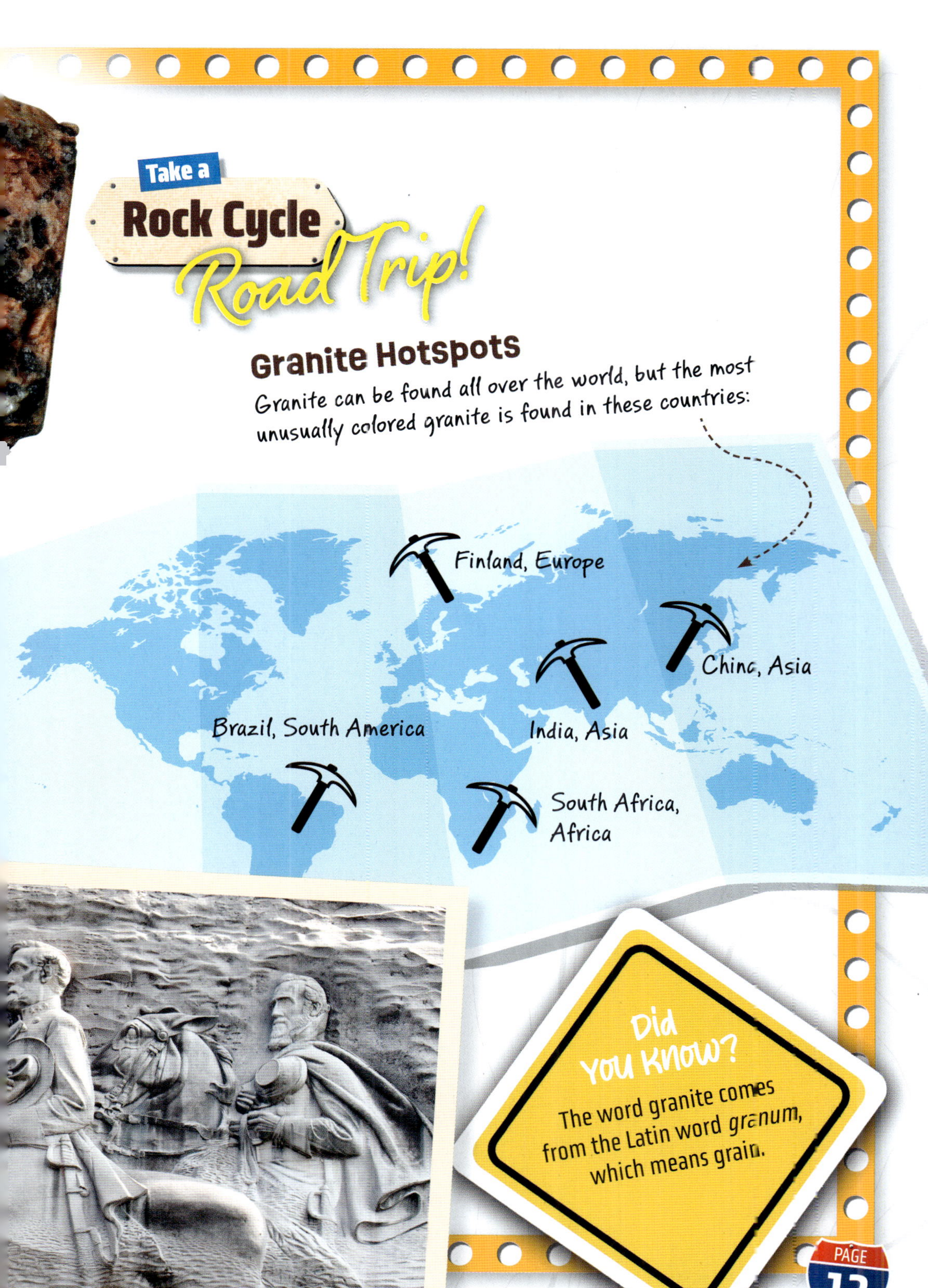
Take a
Rock Cycle
Road Trip!
Granite Hotspots
Granite can be found all over the world, but the most unusually colored granite is found in these countries:
Finland, Europe
China, Asia
India, Asia
Brazil, South America
South Africa, Africa
Did You Know?
The word granite comes from the Latin word *granum*, which means grain.
PAGE
13

Gemstone Factory

The most valuable and biggest gemstones on Earth are often found in the jewelry of rich, famous, or royal people. Many gemstones were made when igneous rocks formed underground. Inside Earth, a gemstone factory is busily producing precious stones.

How Gemstones Are Made

Gemstones mostly form because of changes in intrusive magma as it cools and turns into igneous rock. Most magma contains water or **dissolved** water vapor, depending on its temperature. This water has dissolved chemicals, such as silica, within it. It also contains unusual **elements**, including beryllium and boron. The magma that takes the longest to cool and harden contains a lot of this mineral-rich water. Large crystals or gemstones, such as emeralds and tourmaline, form in this magma.

Bubbling Magma

Gemstones sometimes form in bubbles in magma. As the magma cools, the mineral-rich water gradually turns into crystals of minerals such as rubies and topaz. Gemstones also form in cracks in cooling igneous rock. Water from the surface trickles underground. There, it warms up and dissolves minerals from magma, creating veins, or lines of crystals.

Emeralds are distinctive green gemstones.

In their natural form, diamonds are a rough shape. They are cut and polished into stones that can be worn as jewelry.

Diamond Elevator

Diamonds are found at different places on Earth's surface, but most formed billions of years ago 100 miles (160 km) underground in intense pressure and heat. They get to the surface in a special type of magma called kimberlite. The magma acts like an elevator, carrying the diamonds higher. People look in or near kimberlite rock to find diamonds.

Digging Deeper

In 1938, 12-year-old Roy Spencer found a large black crystal in Australia, which his family used as a doorstop for many years. They later realized it was a rare black star sapphire. The crystal structure in the sapphire reflects a star of light. This black star of Queensland is the world's largest sapphire and is worth tens of millions of dollars!

Chapter 3

Rising Up

If you squeeze a tube of toothpaste, it spurts out of the top. Great pressures underground push lava out of Earth's surface in the same way. This forms extrusive rocks.

Path Through Plates

Magma rises in natural gaps between the plates of Earth's crust. The crust is a little like a cracked eggshell on a hard-boiled egg, where pieces of shell can be pressed together or pulled apart. In places where plates are pulled apart, rock is thinner and the magma can melt a path through the thin rock to the surface.

Wrinkly Clues

At Earth's surface, minerals in the lava quickly cool and become harder. They form very small crystals in the rock. Most extrusive rock is a black rock called basalt. On land, the top layer of lava cools first over the runnier lava beneath, rather like the wrinkly skin on cooling rice pudding! Ropy lavas are igneous rocks that resemble ropes because the wrinkles have turned to stone.

Beneath Earth's surface, its plates fit together a little like the pieces of a jigsaw.

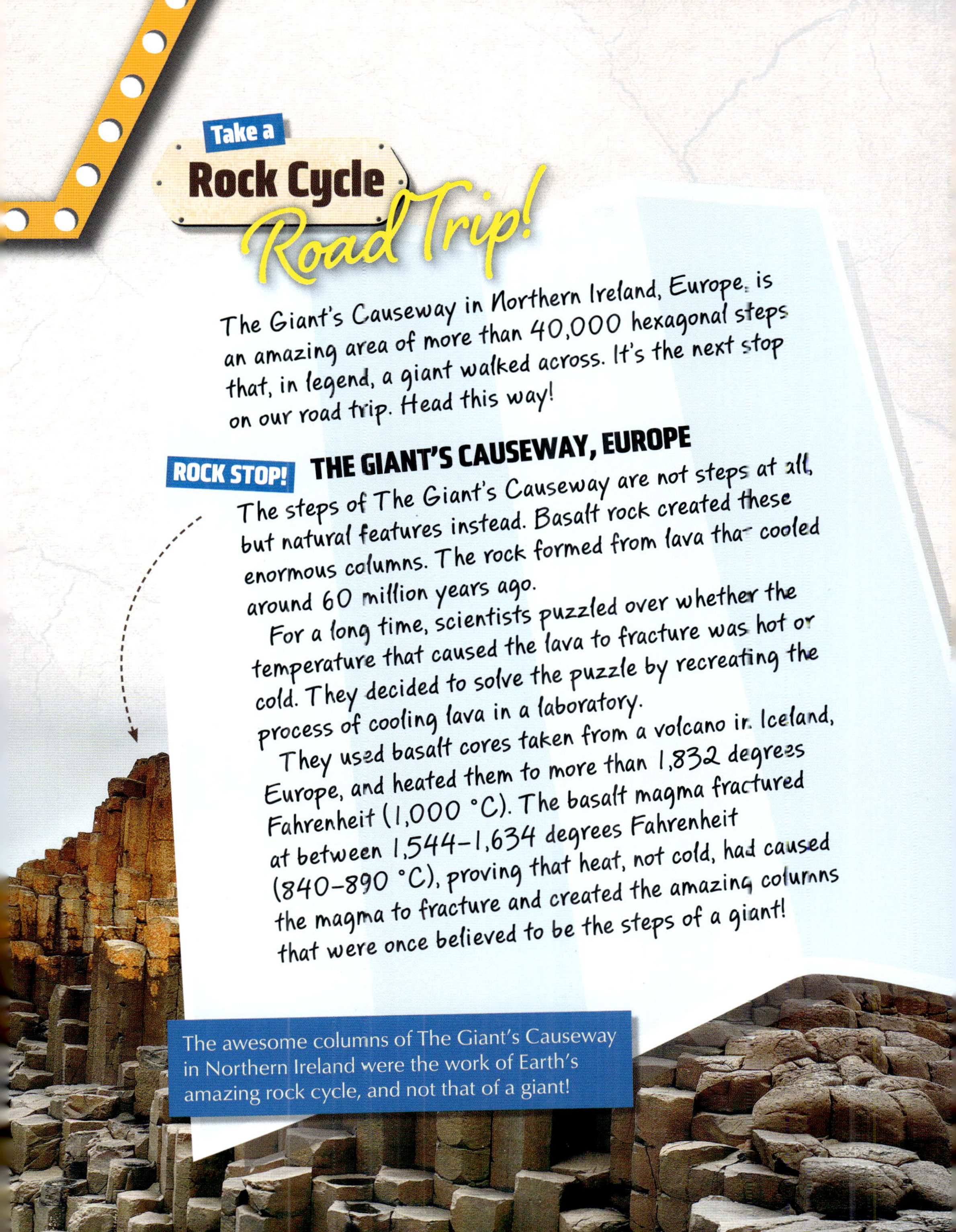

Take a Rock Cycle Road Trip!

The Giant's Causeway in Northern Ireland, Europe, is an amazing area of more than 40,000 hexagonal steps that, in legend, a giant walked across. It's the next stop on our road trip. Head this way!

ROCK STOP! THE GIANT'S CAUSEWAY, EUROPE

The steps of The Giant's Causeway are not steps at all, but natural features instead. Basalt rock created these enormous columns. The rock formed from lava that cooled around 60 million years ago.

For a long time, scientists puzzled over whether the temperature that caused the lava to fracture was hot or cold. They decided to solve the puzzle by recreating the process of cooling lava in a laboratory.

They used basalt cores taken from a volcano in Iceland, Europe, and heated them to more than 1,832 degrees Fahrenheit (1,000 °C). The basalt magma fractured at between 1,544–1,634 degrees Fahrenheit (840–890 °C), proving that heat, not cold, had caused the magma to fracture and created the amazing columns that were once believed to be the steps of a giant!

The awesome columns of The Giant's Causeway in Northern Ireland were the work of Earth's amazing rock cycle, and not that of a giant!

BASALT

What a Rock Star!

Basalt is a fine-grained igneous rock. It most commonly forms as an extrusive rock from lava flows. More basalt lies directly beneath Earth's surface than any other type of rock.

Rock Star Characteristics

- Has fine grains
- Dark gray or black in color
- Can have a shiny, glassy surface

THAT ROCKS!

A lot of basalt is found on the Moon. That is because much of its surface is covered with once-active volcanoes. Olympus Mons is a volcano on the surface of Mars that formed from basaltic lava. It is the highest mountain on the planet and the largest known volcano in our Solar System.

Did You Know?

Basalt has also been found on the planet Venus. It has even been discovered on a large **asteroid** called Vesta. The existence of the rock on other planets, the Moon, and asteroids tells us that other parts of our Solar System have experienced volcanic activity.

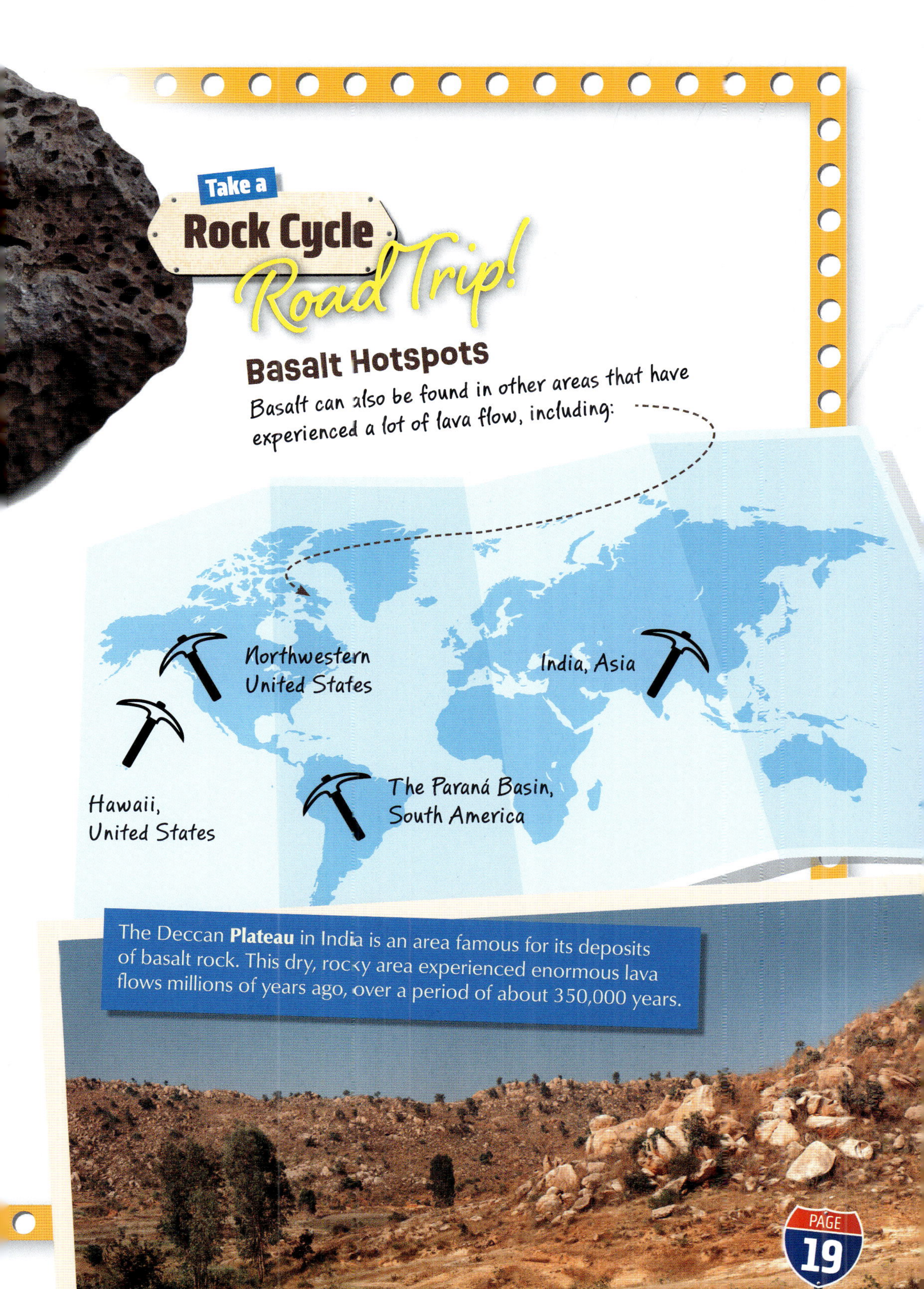

Basalt Hotspots

Basalt can also be found in other areas that have experienced a lot of lava flow, including:

The Deccan **Plateau** in India is an area famous for its deposits of basalt rock. This dry, rocky area experienced enormous lava flows millions of years ago, over a period of about 350,000 years.

The Pressure Builds

Many extrusive rocks form where volcanoes explode. A volcano is a vent, or hole, in Earth's crust that reaches down to a **reservoir** of magma many miles underground. The magma from a reservoir under a volcano does not trickle out of a vent all the time. The magma that rises to the top hardens and blocks the top of the vent. As more magma and gases rise up toward the top of the sealed vent, they push against the surface. In some volcanoes, the pressure builds up so greatly that the magma suddenly breaks through the surface and an eruption occurs.

READ Here

Digging Deeper

The largest volcanic eruption in history happened on the island of Krakatau, Indonesia, on August 27, 1883. It was so powerful that the blast destroyed two-thirds of the island. The blast could be heard more than 2,800 miles (4,500 km) away in Australia.

Since the explosion in 1883, the volcano on Krakatau has grown again, and many scientists think that it may erupt again in the future.

Cones and Shields

Volcanoes have different shapes depending on the types of lava that they contain. Cone volcanoes have tall, steep mountainsides. They form from layers of rock that pile high around the vent after sticky lava eruptions. Shield volcanoes are shaped like flattened hills. They form when runny lava spreads out quickly and forms flatter structures.

Magma Plugs

The most explosive eruptions in the natural world happen when volcanoes are heavily blocked with very sticky magma. Pressure builds up behind the block. Eventually, the pressure becomes too much as the volcano explodes. The lava flows shoot out and form some of the world's most amazing igneous rocks.

Making Bombs

Eruptions shatter the solid rock blocking the vent into jagged pieces that fly into the air. These chunks fall and can stick together, along with lava or fallen ash, to make a type of rock called breccia. Strange circular rocks near an eruption site are volcanic bombs. These formed when lava blobs shot upward and then fell back down to Earth.

Lava bombs can be enormous and are spectacular to see, like this lava bomb on the island of Tenerife, off the coast of Africa.

Ash in the Sky

Sometimes the force of the hot gases shooting from a volcano can turn magma into lightweight and unusual rocks. Lava can explode into tiny pieces that cool and fall to Earth as ash. When ash builds up and hardens, it forms a rock called tuff. Small blobs of silica-rich lava fly into the air and cool very rapidly. They solidify, or become solid, and fall to Earth as hard droplets or even thin hairs of natural glass called obsidian.

Bubbling Gases

On some coastlines around the world, the waves bring in pieces of white or gray rock that float on the water. Pumice floats because it contains bubbles of volcanic gases. The bubbles became trapped inside the rock when it formed. Finding pumice in floating pieces, or in layers under the soil, proves there was once a volcanic eruption nearby.

In legend, the Hawaiian fire goddess, named Pele, lives inside the Kilauea volcano. Thin strands of glass created by molten lava have been called Pele's hair. Tiny pieces of molten lava that have quickly cooled into glassy tear-shaped drops are called Pele's tears.

Take a Rock Cycle Road Trip!

Hawaii is a chain of islands in the Pacific Ocean. The islands formed where magma rose to the surface over thousands of years. In parts of Hawaii, more than 700 gallons (2,650 l) of lava pour out from beneath Earth's surface each second!

ROCK STOP! HAWAII, PACIFIC OCEAN

The Hawaiian Islands began as a volcanic eruption on the floor of the Pacific Ocean about 5 million years ago. Many more eruptions over time continued to build up layer upon layer of lava flows, which cooled to form basalt. The layers of rock eventually reached the ocean's surface, and the youngest island—Hawaii Island (or Big Island)—formed about 300,000 years ago.

Hawaii Volcanoes National Park is home to two of the biggest and most active volcanoes on the planet. They are called Mauna Loa and Kilauea. Both are shield volcanoes. Mauna Loa means "Long Mountain." The volcano is the biggest in the world at 13,677 feet (4,169 m) above sea level. Kilauea means "Much Spreading." It is the world's most active volcano. It stands 4,090 feet (1,247 m) high. It is the youngest volcano on the islands.

Many igneous rocks can be seen in Hawaii, and the islands have both white and black sand. The black sand is made of basalt.

PUMICE

What a Rock Star!

Pumice is an amazing rock—it can float on water until it becomes too waterlogged to stay on the surface. Sometimes, large amounts of pumice created by island or underwater volcanic eruptions will float on the surface, where they are pushed about by wind.

Rock Star Characteristics

- Often light in color, ranging from white, cream, blue or gray, but can be green-brown or black
- Has large, clear holes in its surface
- Rough and **abrasive** to the touch

This jet-skier is circling a large area of floating pumice rocks off the coast of Japan. The pumice was created by an underwater volcanic explosion. Pumice is often found in areas around the Pacific Ring of Fire (see page 27), which experiences a lot of volcanic activity. Japan lies on the Ring.

THAT ROCKS!

Some of the rock that the **Romans** used to build the Pantheon, in Rome, was pumice. The building was completed in around 126 CE.

Did You Know?

When large areas of pumice rock float on the surface of the ocean it is called a "pumice raft." These huge rafts of floating rock are so big that they can be tracked by satellites in space and even pose a threat to ships that sail nearby.

Take a Rock Cycle Road Trip!

Pumice Hotspots

A lot of pumice is found in Europe, particularly in these countries:

Iceland

Germany

Hungary

Italy

Turkey

Greece

Chapter 4
An Igneous World

Our planet's crust is mostly made from igneous rock. Much of this is buried underground beneath another type of rock—sedimentary rock. This is rock that has formed from pieces of weathered and eroded rock.

Mountain Maker

Enormous chunks of intrusive rocks form most of the world's mountain ranges. Igneous rock is very hard and is not easily weathered. It also remains intact during major movements such as the stretching of Earth's crust. Mountain ranges also form as plates shift and shove up igneous rocks that were beneath the surface before the shift. One example is the Sierra Nevada, in the western United States, with its famous peaks including Half Dome and El Capitan.

A lot of basalt rock is found in the volcanic region of Chaîne des Puys in France, Europe.

Volcano Zone

More than half of the world's volcanoes are found around the edge of the Pacific Ocean, in the Ring of Fire. This is where the enormous plate that lies under the Pacific Ocean meets six other plates. Around the Ring of Fire, magma constantly reaches or nears the surface. The Ring is also where most of Earth's earthquakes happen. An earthquake is the shaking of the ground caused when plates push into, rub against, and slide past each other.

Europe has a violent, volcanic history, with some areas still active today. **Dormant** volcanic areas tell the story of the continent's dramatic past, and one of the best places to see this is the Chaîne des Puys in France, which was created mainly during one enormous volcanic eruption. It's the next stop on our road trip!

ROCK STOP! CHAÎNE DES PUYS, EUROPE

The Chaîne des Puys is an area of more than 80 dormant volcanoes. The volcano range is approximately 25 miles (40 km) long and 2 to 3 miles (3 to 5 km) wide. The volcanoes in the range are quite young, with the first eruption happening about 100,000 years ago. The most recent eruption occurred around 6,000 years ago.

The Puy de Dôme is the tallest volcanic peak in the Chaîne des Puys area. It is about 4,900 feet (1,493 m) high.

This extrusive igneous rock formed in the Teide National Park in Tenerife, a volcanic island off the coast of Africa.

Rocks as Resources

People use igneous rock as a **resource**. People **mine** for the rocks they need. Sometimes, intrusive rock is revealed following weathering and erosion. New extrusive rock is found at the surface of volcano sites.

Hard Rocks to Mine

Intrusive igneous rocks with large crystal structures are very hard. People often use explosives to mine these rocks from **quarries**. They drill vertical holes at the top of a cliff face and set explosives in them. By exploding all the holes at once, they can make a large chunk of rock fall off the cliff face. Volcanic rocks with smaller grains are slightly softer, so people can cut and break off pieces using powerful diggers.

Rock Detectives

People often search for igneous rocks because they give clues about the location of valuable materials, including gemstones and ores. Ores are concentrated amounts of metal minerals, such as copper and gold. They are often found as veins within igneous rocks. That is why **geologists** search for kimberlite rock—they know that by digging down into it or sifting through eroded stones from it, they may find diamonds.

READ Here

Digging Deeper

Not only are rocks important for people, but they are also vital resources for other living **organisms** too. For example, rocks are part of important **ecosystems**. They provide habitats, or homes, in which plants and animals can live. An example of the importance of igneous rock are the cliffs at Grand Canyon National Park in Arizona. The cliffs of the Park provide homes for endangered condors and soil **nutrients** for redwood, the tallest trees in the world.

The cliffs of the Grand Canyon National Park provide condors with safe places in which to build their nests and raise their young.

Tough Rocks

Some igneous rocks are among the toughest rocks on the planet. This makes them ideal for use as strong and durable materials. The toughest ones include intrusive granite and gabbro, and extrusive basalt.

Glittering Granite

Granite is often used for polished decorative surfaces, ranging from countertops and stonework on buildings to headstones. Polishing reveals the rock's beautiful crystal structure. Granite withstands normal weathering for a long time, so it stays tough and continues to look good. However, after very long periods, weathered granite crumbles as the crystals come apart.

Crushed and Broken

Granite, gabbro, and basalt are all broken into pieces and crushed to use in supporting roles. For example, crushed stone is used to support railroads or made into **asphalt** used to build roads. Larger chunks are piled up along coasts to prevent sea erosion. These rocks are heavy and strong, so they stay in place and endure great forces without moving.

Sand Survivor

Most of the sand on beaches worldwide is made from tiny grains of quartz that were once inside granite. Over thousands of years, the feldspar and mica minerals in granite weathered and eroded into clay, but the tougher quartz remained in larger pieces. Rivers and oceans carried the sand away, then deposited, or dumped it, on beaches.

When you look closely at sand, you can see that it is made up of many tiny pieces of rock.

Take a

Rock Cycle Road Trip!

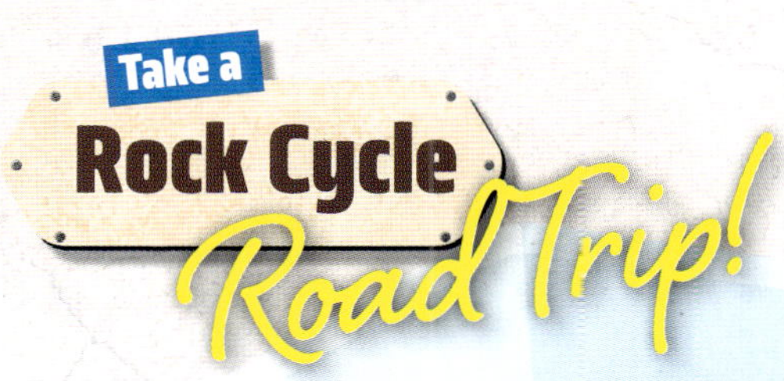

One of the most famous granite sculptures in the country is that of the four US presidents at Mount Rushmore, South Dakota. It's the next stop on our road trip!

ROCK STOP! MOUNT RUSHMORE, NORTH AMERICA

The heads were carved into the cliff between 1927 and 1941 by Gutzon Borglum and his son Lincoln. The artists planned to sculpt the presidents' upper bodies, too, but ran out of money to complete the project.

The granite that the presidents are sculpted from began to form about 1.6 billion years ago, when a huge mass of molten rock began to rise from deep within Earth's crust. As it cooled underground, it formed the granite that makes up much of the Black Hills of South Dakota, where Mount Rushmore is found. The granite that forms the upper part of Mount Rushmore is finely grained, which makes it perfect for carving.

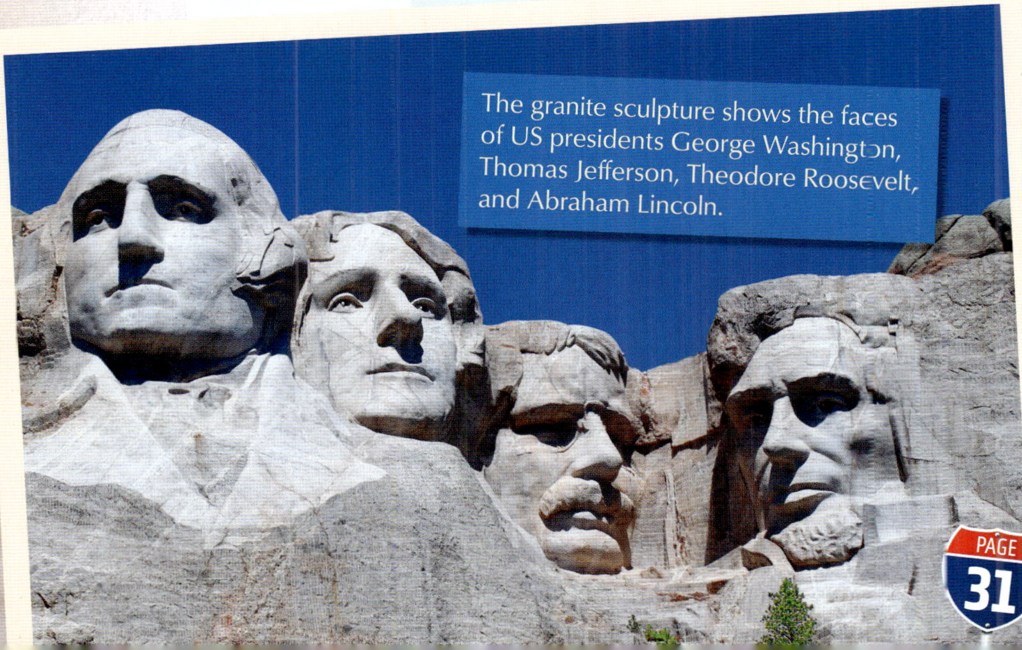

The granite sculpture shows the faces of US presidents George Washington, Thomas Jefferson, Theodore Roosevelt, and Abraham Lincoln.

GABBRO

What a Rock Star!

Gabbro is the most widely found rock in Earth's deep **oceanic crust**. The upper part of the oceanic crust is mainly basalt. Gabbro is made up of the same type of molten rock as basalt but has very different grain sizes.

Rock Star Characteristics

- Usually black or dark green in color
- Has large grains
- Can be polished to create a gleaming, brilliant black surface
- Withstands weathering and erosion well

A lot of gabbro is found in the Columbia River area of Washington and Oregon.

THAT ROCKS!

When magma near Earth's surface cools, the crystals that form in rock are usually small in size. That is because the magma cools and hardens quickly. When magma cools deeper underground, the crystals are surrounded by warmth, and are larger because they form over a longer period.

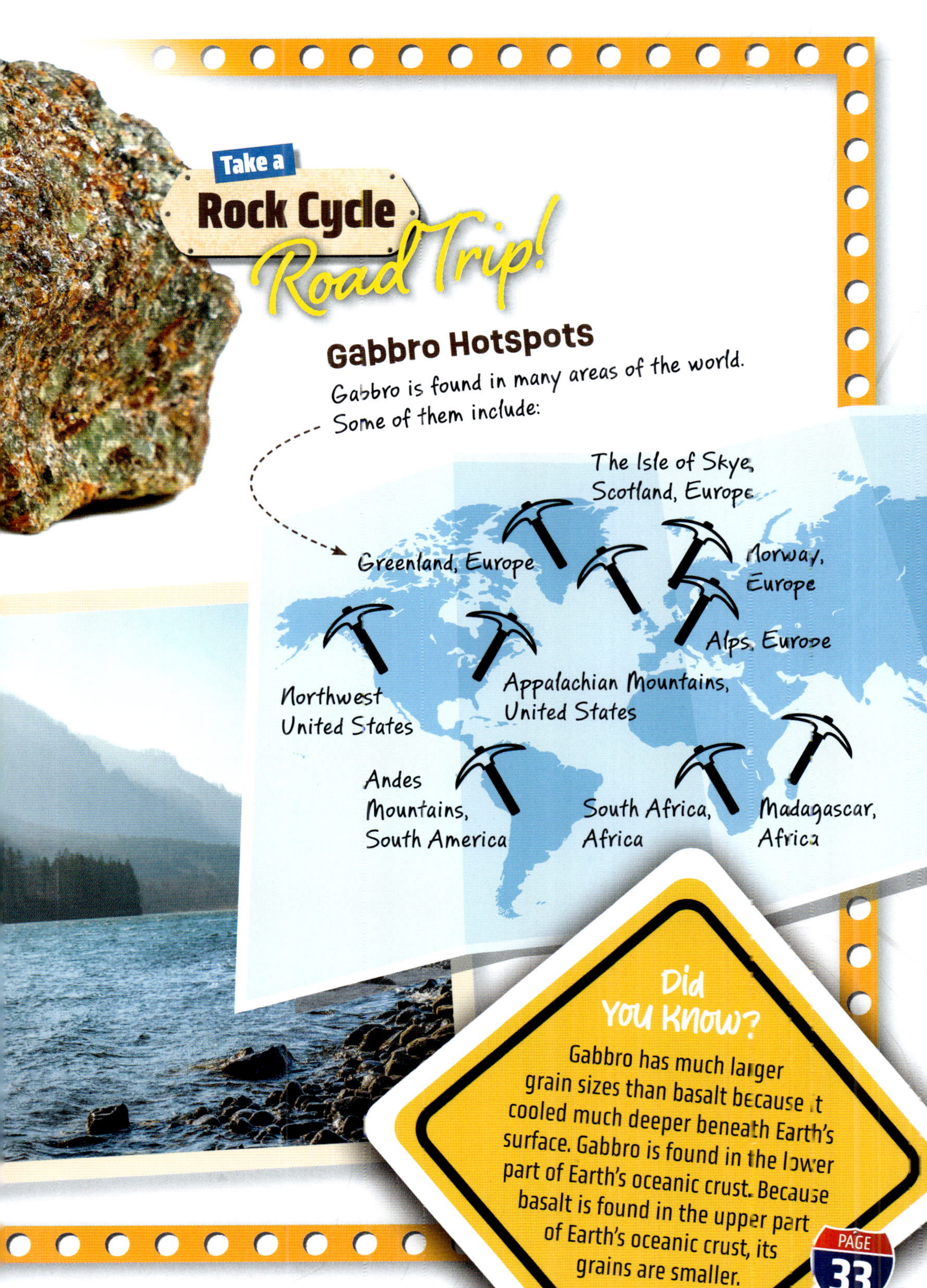

Take a
Rock Cycle Road Trip!

Gabbro Hotspots

Gabbro is found in many areas of the world. Some of them include:

Did You Know?

Gabbro has much larger grain sizes than basalt because it cooled much deeper beneath Earth's surface. Gabbro is found in the lower part of Earth's oceanic crust. Because basalt is found in the upper part of Earth's oceanic crust, its grains are smaller.

Jeans from Rocks?

Did you know that some igneous rocks are used to make faded blue jeans and knife blades? Volcanic extrusive rocks are rarely as tough as intrusive rocks, but they are very **versatile** and have many different uses.

I bet you never knew that blue jeans could be made using pumice stone!

Wearing Pumice

Pumice is widely used as a gentle abrasive. Some people use pumice to rub the hard skin on their feet to make it smooth. New blue jeans are washed with pumice lumps to give them a worn appearance. Most pumice is used because it can be ground into a powder, then mixed with cement and made into light concrete blocks used for building.

Take a Rock Cycle Road Trip!

On a tiny volcanic island in the middle of the Pacific Ocean stand more than 1,000 humanlike statues, made of rock. The island is called Easter Island and it's the next stop on our road trip. Head this way!

ROCK STOP! **EASTER ISLAND, PACIFIC OCEAN**

The statues on Easter Island are between 6 and 30 feet (2 and 9 m) tall and have giant heads. They are called the Easter Island statues, or moais. The statues were carved from an igneous rock called tuff and were first created more than 500 years ago by the island's local people, the Rapa Nui. Tuff forms when volcanoes blast magma, rock, and ash into the air. The material then falls back to the ground, where it cements into rock.

Razor-Sharp Obsidian

Obsidian often looks like shiny black glass but can also be reddish-brown, green, or have gold or silver sheens. This rock has no visible crystals and it can be broken along smooth, curved lines like regular glass. Broken edges can be as sharp as razors, and in the past obsidian was used to make knives and arrowheads. Obsidian blades are still sometimes used today for surgery, but are more often made into gemstones for jewelry.

Some of the statues on Easter Island were given white coral eyes with obsidian pupils. The eyes are no longer present on the statues.

OBSIDIAN

What a Rock Star!

Obsidian forms when molten rock cools so quickly that crystals do not have time to gather and grow. The result is a volcanic glass with a very smooth surface.

Obsidian has been found in the Central Rift Valley in Kenya, Africa. The Rift Valley has experienced a lot of volcanic activity, which caused the black rock to form there.

Rock Star Characteristics

- Usually black in color but can be brown, tan, green, and sometimes blue, red, orange, or yellow
- Very hard but is easy to split into sharp pieces that can be used as tools
- Has very sharp edges

THAT ROCKS!

Gold sheen obsidian is black or brown with tiny golden streaks or dots. When viewed through a microscope, it is clear to see that the streaks or dots are lines of tiny bubbles. The bubbles were made by hot steam from a volcano, and then trapped inside the rock when the obsidian formed.

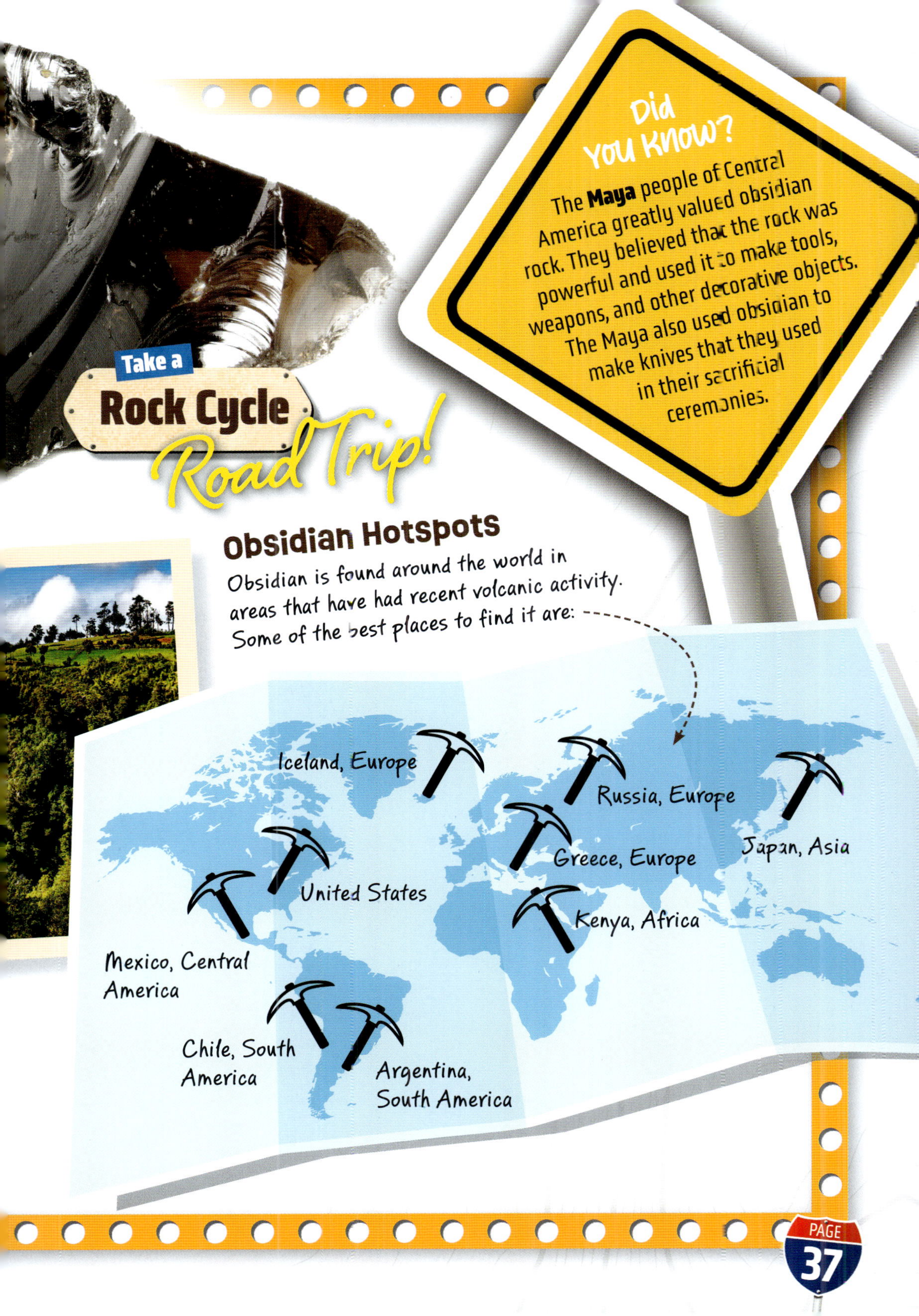

Obsidian Hotspots

Obsidian is found around the world in areas that have had recent volcanic activity. Some of the best places to find it are:

Mount Etna is found on Sicily, an island off the coast of southern Italy, Europe. It can be seen in the distance in this photograph. In the foreground are rows and rows of grapevines.

Living With Volcanoes

Life near volcanoes can be both good and bad. Volcanoes bring useful minerals to Earth's surface and volcanic heat provides people with an **energy source**. However, eruptions can be very dangerous.

Danger Watch

There are around 1,350 potentially active volcanoes worldwide, about 500 of which have erupted in the past 100 years. Eruptions can be fast and deadly if hot gases, ash, and bombs shoot from them. Even the slowest lava flows can knock down and burn everything in their path. Scientists carefully monitor active volcanoes. They also work closely with governments to help keep people safe.

Food-Making Volcanoes

Volcanoes can help us grow food! Many people live near volcanoes because the surrounding soil is rich in nutrients that help them grow crops. Rock formed by volcanoes is rich in minerals from deep in Earth's crust. Over time, these weather to become part of soils around volcanoes. The minerals help crops grow large, strong, and produce a lot of fruit or vegetables.

READ Here

Digging Deeper

Some of Italy's best tomatoes, grapes, and vegetables grow in the dark volcanic soils formed from past eruptions of Mount Etna, which is found in southern Italy, Europe. Head to North Island in New Zealand and you'll find a volcanic landscape that is famous for its farms. The island is green and lush owing to its rich, deep volcanic soil. The soil formed from volcanic ash that was weathered by the island's warm temperatures and plentiful rain. The area is famous as the heart of New Zealand's dairy industry, and many kiwifruits eaten worldwide come from there.

Volcano Power

Near volcanoes the crust is often thin enough for magma to come to the surface. It heats surface water that trickles underground, causing hot springs and **geysers** to form. People use the heat from springs and geysers for energy. They also pump water deep underground to heat it up and use the very hot water to make electricity, or to warm buildings, glasshouses, and swimming pools.

Many people enjoy bathing and swimming in the naturally warm waters of Iceland, which are heated by volcanic activity underground.

Rocks in the Making

Igneous rocks make up about 15 percent of Earth's land surface, and about 95 percent of the upper 10 miles (16 km) of the planet's crust is made up of igneous rocks. They are fascinating because they are the only rocks we can actually see being formed, when volcanoes erupt. Other igneous rocks are formed deep underground, but we can study how they have formed when intrusive rocks come to Earth's surface.

Clues to the Past

Igneous rocks are a direct link to the incredible world inside Earth. For example, elements in some minerals gradually change over time, at a regular rate. Scientists can measure the elements in minerals to figure out the age of rocks. This is easiest in igneous rocks because all the crystals in them are the same age and formed from the same magma. Unlike igneous rocks, sedimentary and metamorphic rocks contain minerals with different ages.

These amazing basalt rock formations are found in Iceland, Europe. If we take care to protect Earth's incredible rock cycle, it will continue creating spectacular igneous rock like this for many years to come.

When we see lava flow across the planet's surface, we are witnessing the formation of igneous rock and the rock cycle in action!

Digging Deeper

In 2014, US scientists measured the age of a tiny crystal of sand from Australia. It formed 4.37 billion years old, making it the oldest piece of Earth ever found. This fragment of igneous rock formed only a few hundred million years after Earth itself first formed. It proves that even at the very beginning of our planet's life, it had a crust. Imagine that: a grain of sand can tell us something about the history of our world!

Rocks Forever?

Although new igneous rock is forming all the time, this process is very slow. We need to keep this in mind when we make use of Earth's rock cycle. Our planet's precious resources must be used with care, including its incredible rocks.

The Road Trip Guide to Rock Hunting

Had a great road trip? Loved the book? Want to try out rock hunting yourself? Awesome! Here's an easy guide that will explain the basics. The great thing about hunting for rocks is that anyone can do it and it costs very little. All you need is a pair of sharp eyes and some resources such as books and websites to help you identify the rocks. A few key pieces of kit help too.

Hammer and Chisel

The rock hunter's most important tools are a hammer and chisel —and it's worth investing in some proper geological ones. The hammer should mostly be used for splitting stones, and not for breaking stones from cliff faces.

A magnifying glass can help you see the detail in a rock. Try to use a glass that provides five to ten times magnification so you can clearly see the rock.

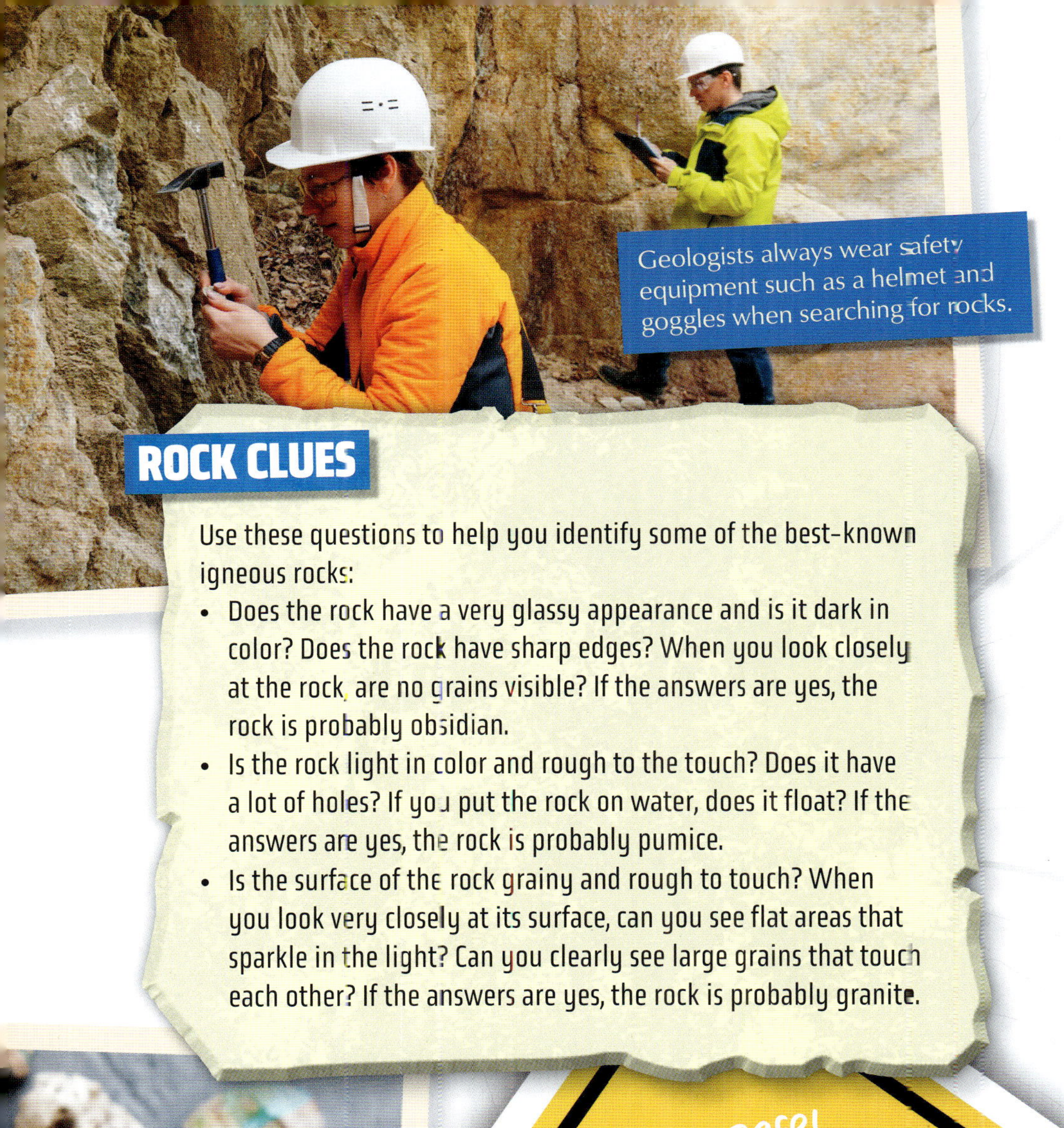

Geologists always wear safety equipment such as a helmet and goggles when searching for rocks.

ROCK CLUES

Use these questions to help you identify some of the best-known igneous rocks:

- Does the rock have a very glassy appearance and is it dark in color? Does the rock have sharp edges? When you look closely at the rock, are no grains visible? If the answers are yes, the rock is probably obsidian.
- Is the rock light in color and rough to the touch? Does it have a lot of holes? If you put the rock on water, does it float? If the answers are yes, the rock is probably pumice.
- Is the surface of the rock grainy and rough to touch? When you look very closely at its surface, can you see flat areas that sparkle in the light? Can you clearly see large grains that touch each other? If the answers are yes, the rock is probably granite.

Keep safe!

Rocks can be sharp, heavy, and hard, and the places where you find them may be dangerous, so it's very important to keep safe. Try to rock hunt in a group and take an adult with you. Rocks can splinter when hit, so always wear goggles when hammering. Tough gloves are useful and a helmet is also important for protection if working near places where rocks could fall.

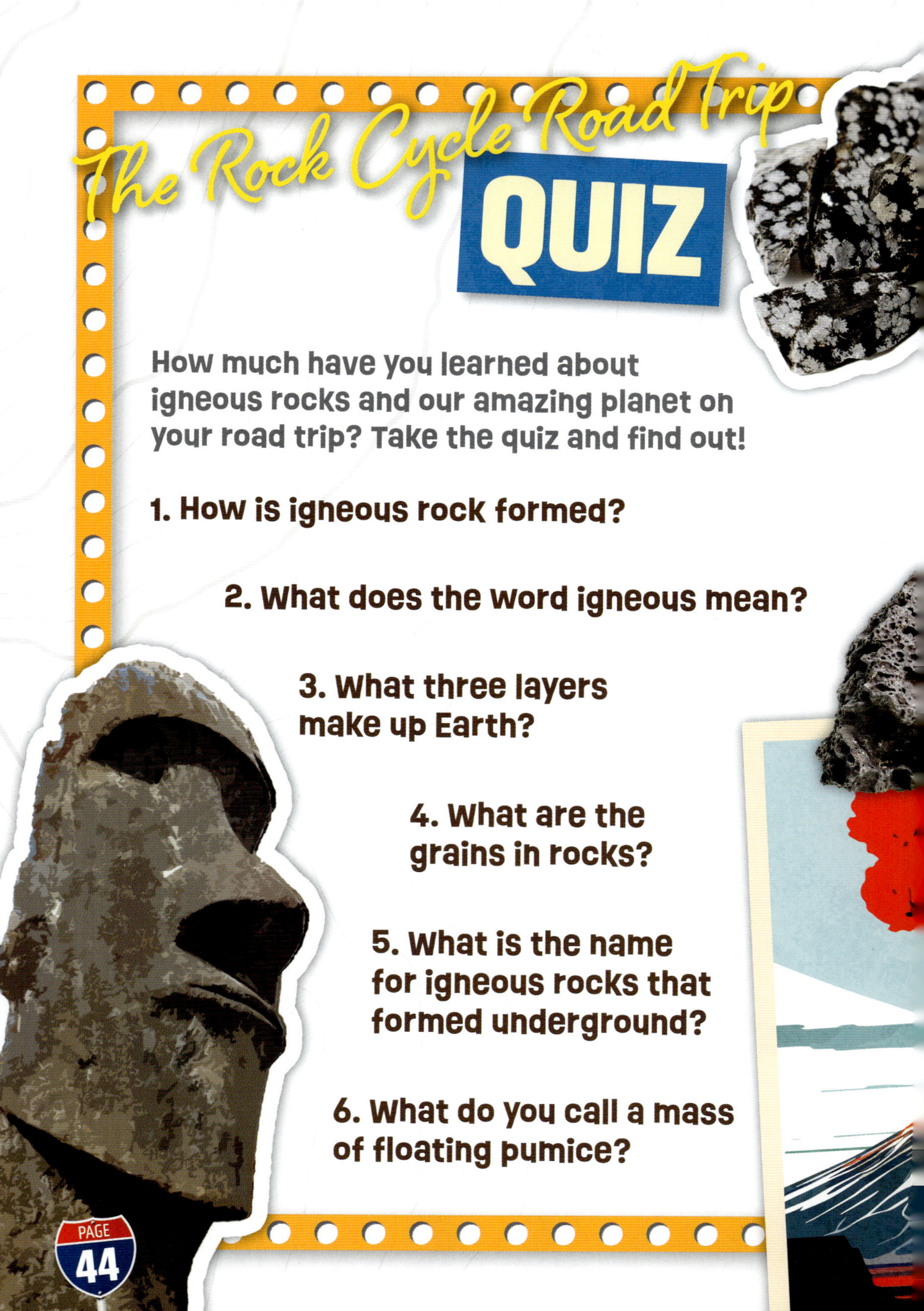

The Rock Cycle Road Trip QUIZ

How much have you learned about igneous rocks and our amazing planet on your road trip? Take the quiz and find out!

1. How is igneous rock formed?

2. What does the word igneous mean?

3. What three layers make up Earth?

4. What are the grains in rocks?

5. What is the name for igneous rocks that formed underground?

6. What do you call a mass of floating pumice?

7. What type of igneous rock forms The Giant's Causeway?

8. What is the name for igneous rocks that formed on Earth's surface?

9. What type of rock makes up Mount Rushmore?

10. Why are there no grains in obsidian rock?

ANSWERS

1. When magma cools and hardens
2. Formed through fire
3. The crust, mantle, and core
4. Crystals
5. Intrusive
6. A pumice raft
7. Basalt
8. Extrusive
9. Granite
10. Because the rock cooled too quickly for grains to form

GLOSSARY

abrasive slightly rough or coarse. Abrasive substances can be used to rub a surface to clean it, or to wear it away

asphalt a sticky, oily substance mixed with small stones and sand, which is commonly used to surface roads

asteroid a rocky object orbiting the Sun, usually found between Mars and Jupiter

crystals minerals that have a very ordered arrangement of atoms in regular, repeating, symmetrical patterns. When we identify rocks, we call the crystals "grains"

dissolved when a solid mixed with a liquid and became part of it, to make a solution

dormant temporarily inactive. A dormant volcano is one that hasn't erupted for a long time, but is expected to erupt in the future

ecosystems all the living things in a particular area and the way they interact with each other and with the environment

elements substances that cannot be broken down into simpler substances by chemical means

energy source a source from which energy can be extracted or recovered. Volcanic regions are a source of heat energy

erosion a geological process in which material is worn away and transported by natural forces such as wind or water

eruption a violent outbreak, such as the eruption of molten rock from a volcano

geologists scientists who study Earth and what it is made of

geysers hot springs that erupt from time to time, sending jets of water and steam into the air

Maya an ancient civilization of indigenous people in Central America

mine to extract a substance from the ground

minerals substances formed by natural geological processes on Earth. All rocks are made from one or more minerals

nutrients substances that provide nourishment for growth

oceanic crust the outer rocky layer of Earth, beneath the oceans

organisms living things, such as plants and animals

plateau a flat area of high ground that rises sharply from the surrounding area on at least one side

pressure a continuous physical force exerted on an object by something it is in contact with. Pressure increases underground, for example, because of the downward push of rock above

quarries large, deep pits from which stone or other materials are extracted

reservoir a natural place where liquid is stored. A reservoir of magma sits beneath a volcano, for example

resource a supply of something that can be used for a particular purpose

Romans the people who lived in Rome, or the Roman Empire, in ancient times

satellite an artificial object placed in orbit around the Sun as an observatory or communication device

Solar System our Sun and the planets and other bodies that orbit it

versatile something that can be adapted and used for many different things

volcanoes vents, or holes, in Earth's crust through which lava, rock, and hot gases can erupt

waterlogged full of water

weathering the wearing away of a substance over time because of the effects of sunlight, wind, water, or other weather conditions

FIND OUT MORE

Fretland VanVoorst, Jennifer. *Igneous Rocks* (Rocks and Minerals). Bellwether Media, 2019.

Pettiford, Rebecca. *Igneous Rocks* (Geology Genius). Pogo Books, 2018.

Rogers, Marie. *Exploring Igneous Rocks* (Let's Rock!). Rosen Publishing Group, 2022.

Take another look at the rock cycle at:
www.cotf.edu/ete/modules/msese/earthsysflr/rock.html

Test your knowledge about rocks at the DK website:
www.dkfindout.com/uk/earth/rocks-and-minerals

This site has information from the US Geological Survey about volcanoes and other activity on Earth:
geomaps.wr.usgs.gov/parks/rxmin/rock.html#igneous

Find out more about igneous rocks at:
studyjams.scholastic.com/studyjams/jams/science/rocks-minerals-landforms/igneous-rocks.htm

Publisher's note to educators and parents:
All the websites featured above have been carefully reviewed to ensure that they are suitable for students. However, many websites change often, and we cannot guarantee that a site's future contents will continue to meet our high standards of educational value. Please be advised that students should be closely monitored whenever they access the Internet.

INDEX

Africa 13, 21, 28, 33, 36, 37
Asia 11, 13, 19, 20, 24, 37

basalt 9, 16, 17, 18–19, 23, 26, 29, 30, 32, 33, 40

core 4, 6
crust 6, 8, 16, 20, 26, 31, 32, 33, 38, 39, 40, 41
crystals 9, 10, 14, 15, 16, 28, 30, 32, 35, 36, 40, 41

elements 14, 40
erosion and weathering 5, 6, 7, 10, 26, 28, 30, 32, 38, 39
Europe 10, 13, 17, 21, 25, 26, 27, 28, 33, 37, 38, 39, 40
extrusive rock 16, 18, 20, 28, 29, 34

gabbro 9, 29, 30, 32–33
gemstones 14–15, 28, 35
granite 9, 10, 12–13, 29, 30, 31, 43

intrusive rock 10, 14, 26, 28, 29, 34, 40

lava 4, 8, 9, 16–19, 21–23, 38, 41

magma 4, 5, 8, 9, 10, 14–17, 20–23, 27, 31, 32, 34, 39, 40
mantle 6
metamorphic rock 5, 40
minerals 10, 14, 16, 28, 30, 38, 40

North America 12, 19, 23, 26, 29, 31, 32, 33, 37

obsidian 9, 22, 35, 36–37, 43
Oceania 15, 20, 39, 41

pressure 5, 6, 15, 16, 20, 21
pumice 9, 22, 24–25, 34, 43

rock cycle 4–7, 17, 40, 41
rock hunting 42–43

sedimentary rock 5, 26, 40
South America 13, 19, 33, 34, 37

temperature 5, 6, 9, 10, 14, 15, 17, 39

volcanoes 8, 10, 11, 17, 18, 20–23, 24, 26–27, 28, 34, 36–41

ABOUT THE AUTHOR

Sarah Eason has written many books for children on a wide variety of topics, from history to geography and science. She would love to take a rock cycle road trip and visit some of the amazing rocky places explored in this book.